Wild Spring

A Spring Stream

Wild Spring

IN PRAISE OF NATURE

Richard Fuller

SWAN·HILL
PRESS

DEDICATIONS

My interests in wildlife started when I was very young and I have been fortunate enough to have had the opportunities to develop them in a practical way. I am also fortunate in having encouragement from friends and family.

Martin Stringer, a keen naturalist and fellow farmer, has accompanied me on many forays, his enthusiasm and knowledge has been an inspiration. Nan Sykes, the outstanding North Yorkshire botanist, has pointed me in the right direction on several occasions and David Holyoak's meticulous research and help in preparing the text of this book has been invaluable.

The support and shared interests of my family has been a source of great fun. Robert, our youngest son, has accompanied me on many trips to wild places, his keen eyes always ready to spot a dragonfly resting in a bog or a golden eagle being mobbed by a merlin high over a distant hill. We are delighted that he is well established as a wildlife artist. David, our eldest son, is also a keen countryman and is following a career in farm management. Then there is the one who holds us all together. The one who deals with the muddy boots and the wet clothes. The one who deals with the moods when the light is not quite right or when the camera batteries run flat miles from anywhere. The one who also loves the countryside, so I dedicate this book to Fran.

Copyright © 1997 Richard Fuller

First published in the UK in 1997
by Swan Hill Press, an imprint of Airlife Publishing Ltd

British Library Cataloguing in Publication Data
A catalogue record for this book
is available from the British Library

ISBN 1 85310 573 2

Typeset by Phoenix Typesetting, Ilkley, West Yorkshire.
Printed in Hong Kong

Swan Hill Press
an imprint of Airlife Publishing Ltd
101 Longden Road, Shrewsbury, SY3 9EB, England.

CONTENTS

INTRODUCTION

Spring is, for me, the most exciting time of the year. The dark winter evenings slowly shorten, the harsh storms abate, the snows melt and the countryside gradually comes to life . . . until eventually during late April and May Mother Nature bursts into frenzied activity.

I have spent all my life living and working on the land. For the last twenty years I have been fortunate enough to manage a thousand acres on the Yorkshire Wolds. During that time I have developed my passions for managing a modern, productive farm and for improving natural habitats within the farming system.

My environmental interests stretch further than the Yorkshire Wolds however. I am very concerned that modern land use, not only by farmers but also by foresters, industrialists and the public for leisure purposes, is putting enormous pressures on the intricate ecology of our countryside. For our environment is indeed fragile. In recent years many habitats have been destroyed, adversely affecting the landscapes and disrupting independent wildlife colonies. Fortunately, there is a greater awareness today of the need to protect our remaining wildlife havens. But sadly, commercial interests and profit are still overriding factors in too many instances. Equally, ignorance of the needs of wildlife species also contributes to the erosion of habitat and the modern urge to sanitise

the countryside destroys vital feeding and breeding resources.

For my part, I have woven into our farming activities a network of habitats which successfully supports a diverse wildlife population. I have proved that by adopting careful planning and management techniques, it is possible to run a hard-headed commercial farming business while promoting landscape and wildlife conservation. Farming must remain prosperous in order to give farmers the opportunities to invest in the countryside and to respond to advice given by conservation organisations such as the outstandingly successful Farming and Wildlife Advisory Group.

My fascination for our natural world has been enhanced by a strong desire to communicate its many wonders, through my photography, to a wider audience. And so, in 1986, I bought a camera and a couple of lenses and set about recording a personal view of some of the species that feed, breed or grow on the farm. Inevitably my photographic hobby extended far beyond the farm's boundaries. Journeys to the remote Outer Hebrides, to Wales and to the high heather moors of Yorkshire have been rewarded with pictures of exciting wildlife.

In this book I have tried to bring you a close-up view of a tiny section of our most precious heritage. I hope these photographs will make people stop and think and wonder. I hope they will help to encourage positive and sympathetic action to secure a future for the natural wonders of our countryside.

OPPOSITE:
A roe deer, large ears listening.

An arctic skua displays on its nesting territory. These birds are masters of the air and they indulge in breathtaking aerobatics as they chase gulls to force them to disgorge their latest meal before stealing it.

FOREWORD

In his first book *GIVENDALE – A Farm in Harmony with Nature*, Richard Fuller described the ways in which he manages a large, highly successful commercial farm with wildlife interests always to the fore, throughout the four seasons.

Here in his second book, he focuses on spring with a further dazzling display of the most superbly evocative photographs and the same memorable prose.

The author is more than a skilled farmer and knowledgeable naturalist; in a very real sense, he is an evangelist on behalf of all those farming and land management practices which ensure that profitable food production goes hand in hand with the maximum diversity of wildlife habitats. He is also a promoter of general care – perhaps cherishing is a more apt word – of the rural environment, both within and without farmland, and through his enthusiasm and dedication is able to stimulate a widening pool of public concern which in turn can bring pressure to bear on those who fashion policy.

WILD SPRING presents a vivid portrait of what is going on throughout Britain from the soft southern countryside to the austerities of the mountains, moorlands and northern coasts during this, the author's favourite season. With remarkable dexterity the book weaves a vast amount of information through word and photograph into an astonishingly compact space. From a range of records of when snowdrops flower to the aggression of skuas on their nesting grounds, and from the relationships between leaf emergence in oaks and the incidence of spring weather, to advice on recreating flower rich meadows, what seems to be the whole panoply of spring is offered to us.

As one of the founding fathers of the Farming and Wildlife Advisory Group dedicated to marrying farming and conservation into an indivisible whole, whose origins go back some thirty years, and as a former chairman of the Countryside Commission and of the Royal Society for the Protection of Birds, I have a profound sense of relief and gratitude when I read a book of this kind. Relief that within the space of thirty years enormous strides *have* been made in achieving conservation objectives; and gratitude for men like the author who have taken up 'the cause' with such solid practical effect and influence.

Few who know anything about environmental issues would, however, quarrel with his concluding analysis that the outlook for protecting our natural heritage is 'rather gloomy'. Much has been done to secure a better understanding of what needs to be done both by policy makers and the general public. And the tempo of progress has been accelerating. But the pressures of a complex industrialised society on a crowded island are unrelenting even when tempered by better perceptions of the problems and their solutions.

Richard Fuller shows us just what is at stake.

Lord Barber of Tewkesbury
Gloucestershire, 1996

THE FIRST HINTS OF SPRING

Late winter is usually the coldest part of the year, despite the gradually lengthening days. It is the season when frosts are most common and snow lies regularly in some parts of Britain, although it is more erratic in others. The harsh conditions prevent plants from making much growth, so they and many of the animals that depend on them are relying heavily on stored reserves.

Most trees and shrubs in the British countryside are without leaves, ensuring that minimal damage occurs from the icy winds which whip through their twigs or the heavy snow which sometimes lies on their branches. These deciduous trees will grow new leaves to manufacture food supplies only when the risk of damage from such severe conditions becomes less. Conifers such as pines and a few of the broadleaves such as holly have a different way of withstanding winter conditions; they grow strong evergreen leaves, which allow them to produce some of their food in all months.

Most smaller plants also remain dormant during the winter. Some annuals survive as seeds waiting to germinate when increased warmth or longer days provide better conditions. Many perennials shed all their leaves and stems from above ground, while others are reduced to low, ground-hugging rosettes of leaves. Very few flowers are to be seen, but that is hardly surprising when the pollinating insects they rely on are hibernating.

Most of the few flowers to be seen in late winter are those that do not require insects for pollination. The dangling catkins of hazel and alder benefit by flowering so early in the year, when strong winds frequently occur and there are no leaves to shield their female flowers from the widely scattered rain of pollen. The earliest flowers on some small herbaceous weeds such as chickweed and groundsel get around the lack of insects by self-pollination within each flower.

By the end of January in the south or during February further north, snowdrops provide a welcome hint of milder conditions to come.

As Flora's breath, by some transforming power,
had changed an icicle into a flower.

(Mrs Barbauld)

The bright yellow flowers of winter aconites often grow amongst the snowdrops, adding splashes of cheerful colour on sunny days.

Apart from an occasional midge, there is little sign of flying insects during the coldest winter months, although a very few species of moths may emerge when the weather relents. Most insects pass the winter as hibernating eggs, pupae, larvae or adults, waiting to renew development or continue activity when conditions improve. It is mainly those living underground, inside wood or beneath accumulations of leaf-litter, that remain active.

The scarcity of active insects during winter requires profound changes in the behaviour of many birds. Most specialised insectivores, such as warblers and swallows, have long since emigrated to spend the winter in warmer countries. But a few, such as goldcrests and treecreepers, continue to hunt for concealed adult insects and their eggs and pupae, although this requires them to spend every daylight hour searching for food. Other birds that are insectivores in summer, such as chaffinches and reed buntings, avoid the food shortages by turning to a seed diet during winter. Many of these small birds abandon any efforts to defend a territory during the winter and hence gain the increased mobility that allows them to flock at rich food sources.

OPPOSITE:
A northerly blast of cold air rushes through a thorn hedge,
forming jagged icicles to add to its many prickly spikes.

Late cold snaps frequently extend winter into spring in the north and east. A heavy hoar-frost clings to this magnificent beech tree. Soon the morning sun will release the ice, sending it crashing to the ground.

This ash woodland will soon launch itself into frenzied activity, but for now it is caught in the grip of a late frost.

A pond waits for warmer times as life is temporarily suspended by the last stab of winter.

Our native thrushes and blackbirds are joined by winter visitors from northern and eastern Europe, including more of their own species as well as redwings and fieldfares. These often rely heavily on the fruits of hawthorn, ivy and other shrubs for winter food, especially when snow cover prevents them from catching worms and insect larvae on grasslands. During good weather in late winter our native blackbirds, song thrushes and robins begin to establish territories in preparation for the forthcoming breeding season, staking out their claims with songs and by threatening intruders. Wintering redwing may also produce bursts of their beautiful whistling song on good days, but all this activity is suspended if hard weather forces them to devote all their efforts to obtaining food.

Many birds benefit from deliberate bird feeding in winter. Besides the house sparrows and starlings that all too readily exploit free pickings of bread, more varied presentations of seed, nuts, dried fruit or fat are helpful to tits, thrushes and finches. Some of the beneficial effects of regular winter feeding apparently extend beyond the hard weather, as is shown by the much higher breeding densities of blackbirds in suburban gardens than in their natural woodland habitats.

As lakes and ponds freeze, food resources rapidly become inaccessible to water and waterside birds. Little grebes, kingfishers, mute swans, herons and snipe are forced to move to feeding grounds on unfrozen streams, rivers or coasts. Besides these local migrants, British estuaries are visited for the winter by many waders, ducks and geese that breed as far afield as Greenland, Spitsbergen and Siberia. The severe Arctic winters necessitate that they make regular migrations to reach wintering grounds with predictable food supplies. Consequently, the survival of these spectacular birds depends on the maintenance of suitable conditions for them not only on their Arctic breeding grounds, but also in their traditional wintering areas. The creation of coastal sanctuaries in which shooting is controlled has done much to protect their wintering areas, so that some, such as barnacle geese, have shown welcome increases in numbers. However, new threats have appeared in the form of proposals to create

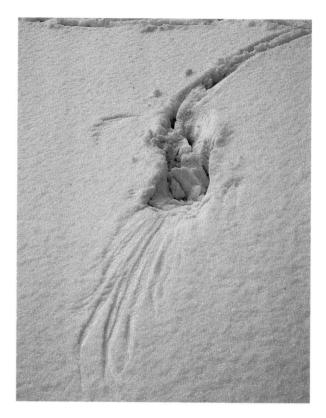

Falls of snow make life difficult for many of our wild creatures. Tracks in the snow aid our knowledge of local animal activity. Here, a cock pheasant has landed, leaving an imprint in the deep snow . . .

barrages which will reduce the areas of intertidal mud on some estuaries.

Changing agricultural practices have had mixed effects on the winter food supplies of different birds. Early ploughing of wheat and barley fields has much reduced the supplies of seed available to finches and geese from stubble fields through the winter. On the other hand, young growth from winter wheat crops provides grazing for wintering brent geese, which have increased in numbers to the extent that they now cause some damage to the crops. The left-overs from potato crops in some parts of Scotland also provide significant food resources for wintering grey geese.

Among our native animals, the insectivorous bats pass the winter hibernating in snug retreats while tiny wood mice continue to forage incessantly beneath the cover of low vegetation, even when it is blanketed by snow. A few others also hibernate, using up their accumulated reserves of fat, including hedgehogs and dormice, but many

. . . But he was soon able to get airborne again.

that are commonly supposed to hibernate, such as badgers and squirrels really remain active, as shown by the tracks they leave in soft snow. Squirrels, like jays and a few other birds, may rely for part of their winter food on caches of acorns or hazelnuts laid down during the preceding autumn. Nevertheless, thick snow cover may reduce the value of these hidden stores by concealing their location, so that the oaks or hazels can also benefit when some of their buried seeds eventually germinate.

Winter is very much the hard time of the year during which fat reserves become depleted, even for those animals which remain active. Grazing hares and deer are forced to rely on the increasingly sparse and old foliage remaining on their food plants; really severe weather may force them to nibble twigs or strip bark. Squirrels also turn to buds and bark, so that they may incur the anger of foresters by damaging trees. Predators such as foxes and sparrowhawks must rely on their hunting skills to catch adult prey that are by now less numerous and perhaps sharper witted than in late summer, although prey weakened by starvation

may provide a welcome bonus when conditions are at their worst.

The progressive increase in day length during late winter and the increasing warmth as the sun rises higher each day gradually lead from winter into spring. Plants develop new growth and begin to flower as they respond to the longer days and greater warmth. The timetable for these changes is a very flexible one. Indeed, the spring equinox in March, or the change to British Summer Time in late March give only the roughest predictions of when spring will or should arrive. This is because regional, local and annual differences can cause the timetable to be shifted by several weeks.

Naturalists often use the development of leaves and flowers on particular plants as a guide to the progress of spring. Pointers to early spring are the opening of the large 'sticky-buds' on horse chestnut trees or the flowering of wood anemones. The flowering of early apple trees, horse chestnuts and lilac announce the main arrival of spring, and the flowering of hawthorn and rowan (mountain ash) mark the end of spring.

The activity of birds also gives a good indication of the arrival of spring. Nesting rooks and the arrivals of early migrant chiffchaffs and wheatears mark early spring, by mid-spring many swallows have arrived and blackbirds are feeding nestlings, and late spring sees the arrival of spotted flycatchers and the nesting activity of goldfinches.

The progress of spring and its variations have long been of interest to naturalists and methods for recording the times of leaf development, flowering and other changes (the science of phenology) have developed over the past 250 years alongside the development of the systematic recording of the weather. As early as 1751 the great Swedish botanist Linnaeus described methods for keeping records in his *Philosophia Botanica*, and these were applied and extended over the following century, especially in central Europe. In Britain, the Marsham family maintained detailed records from 1736 to 1925 on their estates in Norfolk. These show, for example, that the first snowdrops to flower were as early as 15 December in 1838 and as late as 19 February in 1895, with an average date of 16 January.

Foam, created by rushing streams, freezes into saucers which whirl around in eddying currents. Slowly, they grow larger as more foam freezes onto their outer rims.

Icicles formed by the splashing waters of a swollen stream.

As the snow melts on the fields, a hare waits patiently for the grass to grow.

Remote northern lochans attract rare breeding birds in spring. The haunting calls of the red-throated divers will soon be heard all over the moorland. The burbling calls of the curlews will announce their arrival, as they lay down their claims to nesting territories.

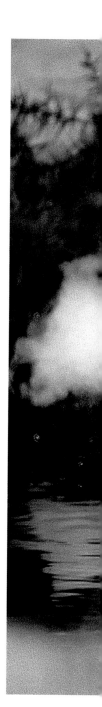

A snipe wades in the slack, unfrozen water at the edge of a stream, where it will find its next meal by probing the soft mud with its long beak.

*High up on the moorland red deer roam. They are lean at
the end of the winter period after futile foraging over sparse,
snow-covered vegetation.*

Strange, yellow brains-fungus is visible from quite a
distance, as it grows on the horny branches of gorse.

The wide-ranging surveys and long historical records show that there is much that is predictable about the progress of spring, as well as some things that cannot be predicted. Regional differences are perhaps the most predictable variations in timing. Spring arrives earlier in southern than in northern Europe, as shown for example by the appearance of the first apple blossom in late March in Portugal, early April in southern France but not until late May in central Sweden. Even within Britain there are appreciable differences between north and south, not only with plants but also with many animals. For example, magpies on average begin laying a week later in northern than in southern England. Such differences as these are easily explained by the longer day length and greater warmth in the south than in the north.

A complicating factor, however, is the effect of the Atlantic Ocean, which leads to marked differences between the mild winters and cool summers of the Atlantic coasts and the cold winters and hot summers of the continental interior. In spring these effects result in earlier seasons along the Atlantic seaboard than far inland, as shown for example by the flowering of the earlier primroses in January in west Cornwall but not until February or March in much of the English Midlands.

Altitude also needs to be taken into account in predicting when spring 'should' arrive. Average temperatures decrease by about one to two degrees Celsius for each 100 metres of altitude, so it is no surprise that mountain areas are late in seeing spring. Furthermore, in steep country the aspects of slopes may be significant. South-facing slopes get the full benefit of the sun's warmth, whereas north-facing slopes may be in shadow for parts of the day, so that plants there receive less warmth and develop later. Similar effects are also evident at a much more local scale, as where the south side of a hedgerow has plants leafing and flowering ahead of those on its more shaded northern side. Even soil types play a part in deciding the timing of plant development: wet, clayey soils are slow to warm so that plants growing in them develop later than those in drier, lighter soils.

A flight of barnacles wheels into their roost, joining gulls and waders on the sands of Loch Indaal.

The Western Isles are renowned for incredible skies. Here, a dramatic sunset over Loch Indaal rounds off a marvellous day's bird watching.

Even when all these predictable regional and local factors are taken into account, there is much unpredictability from year to year in the timing of spring. In Britain it is the unpredictable weather associated with our position on the Atlantic seaboard of Europe that accounts for these uncertainties. The most important factor in the weather which varies from year to year is undoubtedly the amount of warmth available for plant growth. Records shows a clear picture of plants responding early and rapidly in unusually warm years but deferring development in cold ones. Predicting the timing of spring's events in detail is therefore as difficult or hopeless a task as predicting its weather!

Problems in predicting spring weather may be serious for the farmer, with the need to balance the aim of getting crops started early to ensure a long growing season against the risk of damage or loss from late frosts. Wild plants and animals face the same problems. An oak tree needs to be in leaf for as many months as possible in order to manufacture its food as a basis for survival, let alone its growth and acorn production. Unfortunately for oaks, when leaf development begins it cannot be reversed, only delayed. If an imaginary oak tree were to take no chances of damage from late frosts by deferring the growth of leaves until say June, then it would grow less than its early-leafing neighbours and perhaps eventually die as they shade it out. On the other hand, if it attempted to grow leaves in February each year it would be assured of frost damage to the leaves so that it would lose valuable growth and it would be at a competitive disadvantage. To balance these conflicting requirements, oaks have therefore become adapted so as to grow their leaves as early as is safe under local conditions. In some years a rapid improvement of the weather means a missed opportunity, in other years a late frost may catch some leaves, but each tree is well adapted to the average of its local conditions.

OPPOSITE: Shafts of sunlight search the earth and breathe life into the woodland floor after a long hibernation.

As the days lengthen, the songbirds start to think about setting up nesting territories. To be successful their feathers must be in good condition. Here, a robin has a 'sort out'.

A jay sits on an old log, wondering where he has left his acorn!

Birds beginning to nest face similar problems. A snap of bad weather during nest-building can easily result in a delay in laying until conditions improve, but when the clutch is laid and the eggs are being incubated the choice is between total abandonment of the nest or attempting to continue through adverse conditions. It is not unusual for a late snowfall to overtake the early nesting attempts of mistle thrushes or blackbirds, so that birds may be found trying to incubate with snow surrounding them. If a thaw comes quickly there may be no problem in this, but more sustained hard weather will lead to the abandonment of the eggs before the adult birds place their own welfare at risk.

It might be thought that blackbirds and mistle thrushes would be better always to defer their first nesting attempts until later in spring. But to do this would result in their first brood of nestlings being reared after the main flush of earthworm and insect food became available. In order to produce as many young as possible, it therefore pays them to begin nesting as soon as the temperature starts to rise, so that their nesting is then at least roughly in time with the changes in vegetation that affect the insect foods they need to feed growing nestlings.

Migrant birds such as swallows face even greater problems in the face of unpredictable spring weather. A long migration from Africa will have depleted their fat reserves and they face a demanding time competing for nest sites. Their arrival on the breeding grounds needs to be timed so that insect foods are already sufficiently plentiful, while they must not arrive so late that all the best nesting sites are already occupied. Again, they are adapted to the average conditions and in most years the timing of their arrival is appropriate. Just occasionally very cold conditions force them to halt on their northward journeys, or even result in the death of the first wave of migrants.

A female reed bunting fluffs out her feathers.

A graceful massing of mute swans at Abbotsbury.

My fascination for the sea and its birds developed when I was very young. I spent my childhood living close to the Menai Straits in North Wales and I used to wander off down the shoreline, watching the birds and observing the porpoises leaping as they travelled through the straits. My mother bought me the Observer's Book of British Birds *and I* used to take it with me on my early bird-watching trips to make sure that I identified the birds correctly. I also used my little book to paint mental pictures of birds such as skuas and gannets flying in wild storms over rocky shores. One day I was walking along the beach when I came across a dead gannet lying on the high-tide line. I stretched its wings out and I remember being in awe of its size and thinking that my little book was right – this huge bird really did exist.

That encounter left a deep impression on me. At the far end of the straits, there is an estuary known as the Foryd where in winter I used to watch huge flocks of ducks, waders and swans. Some thirty-five years later, I photographed a group of mute swans there, silhouetted in the sunset. It was also some thirty-five years later that I started to make trips to those wild places to watch the skuas and the gannets flying over rocky shores, and my childhood visions were realised.

EARLY SPRING

The change from winter to spring is nowhere more striking than in woodland. Within weeks the quiet winter scene of bare trees above brown leaf-litter has been transformed: buds burst to reveal new growth, the ground is studded with wild flowers and birdsong fills the air.

Most of Britain had a woodland cover around 6,000 years ago such that 'a squirrel could travel from Kent to Scotland without ever touching the ground' and this 'climatic-climax vegetation type' would still exist were it not for the hand of man. Woodland has existed continuously on some of the sites of this primeval forest, leaving us with precious fragments of so-called ancient woodland that are especially rich in wildlife. Elsewhere, newer plantations on previously cleared ground have been recolonised by woodland plants and animals and the best of these are also rich in wildlife, unlike those that are devoted entirely to closely planted conifers.

The predominant trees of our native woods are oaks, just as they were in the forests of 6,000 years ago. On the poorer soils and steeper slopes, such as in the Welsh valleys, the commonest oak is the sessile oak. On richer soils we find mainly pedunculate oaks. Both species, but especially the pedunculate oak, support very large numbers of insect species on which woodland birds depend.

Other trees that form natural woodlands more locally include beech and ash, which prefer chalky areas, while wych elm and alder are characteristic of wet ground. Scots pine is thought to be native only in Scotland. Birches are often conspicuous colonists on ungrazed heathland and other bare ground, but most birch woodland will eventually give way to oaks if natural succession continues unimpeded. Added to these trees are some tall shrubs which may form a conspicuous part of native woodlands, especially hazel, and a variety of introduced trees of which sycamore is both the oldest established and most plentiful.

Man has managed and exploited woodlands over many centuries, so that scarcely any of the woodland we now have can be regarded as fully natural. The removal of timber and dead wood, the planting of both native and exotic trees, coppicing to produce stakes and the grazing of the woodland floor have all had important influences on the structure and composition of our remaining woodlands. Coppicing allows more light to reach the woodland floor and benefits many plants and butterflies, as does the creation of woodland clearings in forestry operations. The removal of old or dying trees is less desirable, since they provide homes for wood-boring insects and food and nest sites for woodpeckers and other birds. The removal of fallen dead wood is also damaging to wildlife as it deprives many small animals such as snails, beetles and woodmice of the micro-habitats in which they shelter.

Woodlands can usually be managed so that they provide a worthwhile forestry crop while benefiting wildlife. Even clear-felling of small areas of deciduous woodland need provide only a temporary setback for woodland wildlife, especially if old tree stumps are encouraged to start new growth, existing saplings are allowed to grow and surrounding areas provide woodland flora and fauna that can recolonise the cleared ground. In the meantime the plants and animals of woodland clearings establish a temporary tenancy, adding to the diversity of the local wildlife. Of course, the permanent clearing of large areas of existing woodland results in the permanent loss of wildlife, as well as of amenity and future timber resources. On the other hand, the planting of new monoculture forests in moorland and mountain areas is generally undesirable because the plants and animals that are lost are of much greater significance than those which colonise the 'new' woodlands.

OPPOSITE:
A clump of green hellebore – a rare plant usually found growing in ancient woodland.

31

Woodcock are early nesters and masters of camouflage – even their brown mottled eggs melt into the background when left unattended.

A dipper carries insects, caught on the bed of a stream, to feed a growing brood of chicks.

Sessile oak woods, clinging to Welsh hillsides, are superb habitats. For their food source, many bird species depend on the multitude of insects and larvae which eat the oak leaves. Summer visitors such as pied flycatchers, wood warblers and redstarts join resident tits to rear their families. Jays feed on the acorns and sparrow-hawks flip between the trees, hunting for small birds to feed their demanding chicks which wait on platforms built high up in the trees. Fortunately, many of these ancient woodlands are now managed as nature reserves or country parks, ensuring protection for their dependent wildlife and for future generations.

Spring in woodland owes much of its charm to the flowers of the woodland floor; favoured places have great sheets of bluebells, banks of primroses or masses of wood anemones. The delicate wood sorrel, violets and the stately early purple orchid can also be found here and there. Most of these flowery riches are concentrated into a few weeks of spring as the plants await sufficient warmth, then rush into flower before the leafy canopy of the trees closes above them to reduce both light and warmth on the woodland floor. After the leafy canopy develops it is mainly the more shade-tolerant plants that still flower.

Each of the flowers of spring woodland has its own range of preferences for soil types, shading and aspect. For example, primroses are at their best on banks on damp, clayey soils, bluebells are very tolerant but like mildly acidic soils, the rare green hellebore and herb Paris both prefer limey soils and dog's mercury is most abundant in undisturbed sites such as those of ancient woodland. Toothwort is a root parasite that grows mainly on hazels but sometimes also on elms, especially on good soils and often over limestones. Others such as red campion prefer edges rather than true woodland, while marsh marigold and opposite-leaved golden saxifrage occur in wet places.

Many of the woodland flowers benefit from coppicing because it allows more light to reach the woodland floor, at least during the early stages after the coppiced trees have been trimmed back. Unfortunately, however, this traditional technique of woodland management is on the decline because, being labour-intensive it is expensive, and because the demand for wooden fence stakes has declined. Several of the characteristic woodland flowers can persist long after woodland has been cleared; for example bluebells often grow well under bracken, or primroses on banks in meadows. Hedgerows and hedgebanks often also provide good habitat for these two species, even in areas where little woodland remains. Plants of the woodland edge such as red campion, cow parsley and brambles have derived even greater benefits from hedgerows in that these strips of artificial habitat have much extended their growing ranges.

A stream flows quietly through a wooded valley. The cold winter spates have now subsided, leaving safe places for dippers and grey wagtails to nest. The wooded banks are dusted with pale greens as new leaves unfurl and the aromas of spring add to the vista of a new beginning.

Early purple orchids, bluebells and wood anemones grow in the ancient ash and hazel woodlands. These unique habitats are now greatly reduced in number because commercial interests in the past have destroyed many of them. The absolute protection of the remaining ones is vital.

Bluebells growing in ancient ash woodland. To ensure the future of such attractive areas the regeneration of the woodland is essential. The control of rabbit populations has a major impact on the survival of seedling trees. If, however, there are too few young trees naturally colonising the woodland, then it may be necessary to clear-fell small areas in rotation and to replant indigenous species.

Sweet violets bend gracefully to early morning sunlight.

A handsome mistle thrush feeds an earthworm to well-feathered chicks. These birds nest early when cold gales blow sleet and snow showers from the north. The chicks survive with their heads down during the storm's rage, safe in the knowledge that their parents had the foresight to tie their home into the elder bush with baler twine.

The strange flower of herb Paris, a rare plant which grows in ancient woodland.

OPPOSITE: Toothwort, a strange parasitic plant growing on the roots of hazel in ancient woodland.

Away from coasts and mountains there are few natural grasslands in Britain. Nevertheless, forest clearance for pastures began around 5,000 years ago when the neolithic colonists occupied the chalklands and some other parts of England and continued on an increasing scale through the Bronze Age and Iron Age, so that by medieval times much of the country was grassland. This long history accounts for the richness of the floras of undisturbed old pastures and meadows. Conspicuously beautiful spring flowers such as cowslips and spotted orchids are accompanied by a wide variety of less conspicuous flowers and grasses, so that as many as sixty species can be identified in a single old meadow.

Unfortunately, the past fifty years have seen the loss of all but a small fraction of the flower-rich grasslands, the losses being greatest of all on the more fertile lowland soils. Ploughing of grassland to increase arable production during the Second World War destroyed many thousands of old pastures and meadows. Of those that escaped, most fell victim to agricultural 'improvement' in the post-war years, as artificial fertilisers became widely used to increase the productivity of grasses. These nitrogen-rich fertilisers boost the growth of rye grass and other grasses desirable to farmers, so that less competitive plants such as cowslips and orchids cannot compete and are lost from the flora.

Some of the richest of the few remaining flower-rich meadows are now carefully managed as nature reserves. These are grazed through the winter, left for hay until very late in the spring and then the aftermath is lightly grazed again. Grazing by cattle is best on rich lowland grasslands, while sheep may be better on poorer grassland; horses tend to graze selectively and cause localised damage to the turf, so they are less desirable. If any fertilisers are added, their use should be limited to light applications of farmyard manure at intervals of several years. With this regime hay production is considerably less than on agriculturally 'improved' fields, but apart from the delights of seeing fields yellow with cowslips or purple with green-winged orchids, many owners now receive more tangible recompense for lost productivity in the form of government grants.

Modern farming methods have pushed cowslips back to marginal, unimproved grassland. However, well-managed woodland margins and roadside verges can support spectacular numbers of this evocative spring flower.

False oxlip. A hybrid between primrose and cowslip, this graceful plant is found wherever both grow together, especially in old woodland.

Some attempts to recreate wild-flower meadows have also met with considerable success, although this is no alternative to protecting the best of the old meadows. After all, recreating a good meadow is a slow process that will show some results after a few years but take decades to succeed fully, especially on the nutrient-enriched soils that are nowadays so widespread. The process of recreating a wild-flower meadow mainly involves sticking to the management regime just described. The use of commercial wild-flower seed mixtures should be very carefully avoided for this or any other purpose, since most contain foreign plants or alien strains of native ones. If natural recolonisation of a meadow is to be enhanced, it is best done by spreading cut hay from a local flower rich meadow onto its surface, so that local plants of the appropriate species are reintroduced.

Insect activity becomes conspicuous on warm days during early spring. Honey bees become active and several species of bumble bee emerge from hibernation and begin to visit pussy-willow catkins, lesser celandines and other early flowers. The bumble bees really are bigger and better at this time of year than most of those remembered from the previous summer, for these are the big fertile queen bees that are establishing and provisioning nests from which the more numerous but small worker bees will later emerge.

The pollinators of spring flowers also include an increasingly varied assortment of flies, beetles and insects of other orders. Long-tongued bee-flies pollinate the deep-throated primrose flowers, while the open cups of wood anemones are accessible to a wider range of flies, as well as to bees and beetles.

The first butterflies may make a temporary appearance on any unusually warm day in late winter, but substantial numbers do not usually appear until early spring. The earliest to appear are usually those that have over-wintered, as hibernating adult insects, especially small tortoiseshells and peacocks. These are sometimes joined by odd individuals of red admiral or painted lady, especially following years in which many of these species have arrived as migrants. One of the first moths to appear in numbers, the herald moth, also over-winters as adults. Not long after these early harbingers of spring, the first broods of several other butterflies emerge from pupae that have over-wintered, including orange-tip, brimstone, large white and small white. All of these soon become conspicuous in places where their food plants grow, namely Jack-by-the-hedge and other wild plants of the cabbage family for the orange-tip, buckthorn or alder buckthorn bushes for the brimstone, but mainly cultivated cabbages for the two whites.

Our native reptiles and amphibians hibernate during the winter. Soon after they emerge at the beginning of spring, common frogs and common toads make their annual journeys to the waters where they spawn. The frogs are content to breed in small groups in ponds or flooded ditches but toads breed in larger groups in big ponds or lakes, sometimes in such large congregations that busy roads nearby become littered with the corpses of unlucky toads heading to and from their chosen lake. In a few places road signs have been erected to request motorists to slow down to avoid the toads and these seem to achieve a certain amount of success, possibly because drivers are curious to see the cause of the unusual road signs.

Only the hardest weather stops the movements and soft nocturnal croaking of frogs and toads at their ponds. The globular masses of frog spawn or strings of toad spawn can often be seen beneath the ice during a cold snap, but little harm seems to come from this and the spawn soon hatches to give masses of swimming tadpoles.

Out on a freshly-sown arable field a lapwing settles onto her four well-camouflaged eggs. This is one of farmland's breeding species which has declined in recent years, due to the increased practice of growing more profitable autumn-sown cereals. In the spring the rapidly growing crops deprive the lapwings of suitable nesting sites. Where spring-sown crops are still grown or where land is set aside under the European Union's Common Agricultural Policy, the birds thrive, albeit on contracted areas. One of the most exciting sounds of spring is the calling of the peewits accompanied by the 'zipping' of air rushing through their wings as they perform aerobatics over their territories, displaying to their mates or chasing off passing carrion crows.

A robin pops a hoverfly into the gaping beak of a fluffy chick.
Many songbirds depend on insects to feed their young and
insects depend on the plants to complete their life cycles and
for food.

An April storm races across the landscape. After it passes, the wet trunks of the trees glisten in the sunlight and sparkling drops of water fall from the branches onto soft, dead leaves lying on the woodland floor. April's lambs gallop from under the shelter of hedgerows watched by anxious mothers, and the birds begin to sing again.

The larch tree is attractive at all times of the year. Often planted as a nurse crop in hardwood plantations, it serves as ideal nesting cover for many songbirds. Its pink flowers resemble tiny pineapples but soon grow into the familiar cones. Eventually, as autumn approaches, the soft green needles turn a rich golden brown. As the hardwoods grow stronger the larch are thinned to be used for fencing posts and rails.

A great crested grebe broods her eggs. Regarded as one of our most graceful waterside birds, they perform spectacular courtship displays, dancing across the surface of lakes before offering vegetation to each other with shaking heads and touching breasts.

A common frog at the water's edge.

*A mallard tries to hide amongst vegetation with her brood of
ducklings, but one gives the game away.*

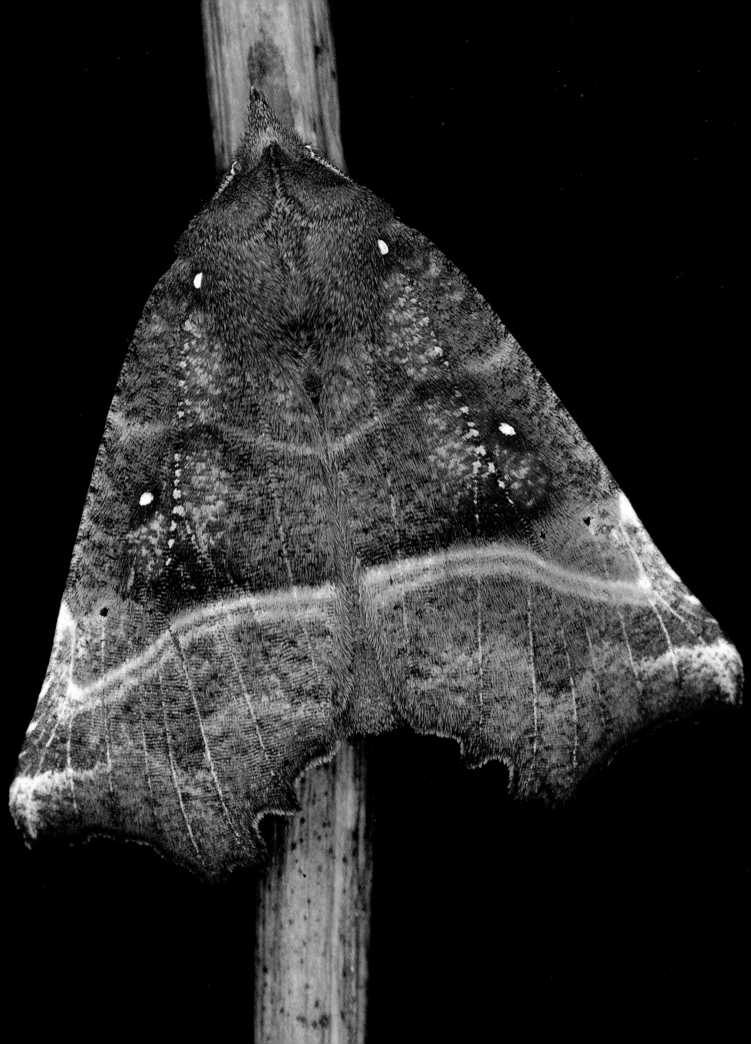

OPPOSITE:
The nocturnal herald moth whose glorious colours are rarely seen by the human eye.

Moorhens are widespread, colonising the smallest areas of fresh water. They are prolific breeders and squabble, often violently, to secure nesting sites. They have bad habits, one of which is killing large numbers of frogs as they try to spawn in ponds.

On heathland our only venomous snake, the adder, is also conspicuous in early spring. Individuals bask in sunny spots with little vegetation to shield them at this time of year, but courting adders attract attention by dancing actively together. They are generally shy and slip away into cover of vegetation when approached, so the slight risk of a nasty bite comes mainly from accidentally treading on them while walking with bare feet or bare ankles.

Birdsong reaches a crescendo during spring, when more individuals of more species sing for longer than at any other time of the year. The reason for this activity is to advertise and defend nesting territories. Singing peaks around dawn and dusk, perhaps because the weak light at these times prevents effective foraging so that time spent singing is not time lost from other activities. Blackbirds have a special dawn song that is fuller, richer and more varied than the song used at other times of the day.

The poetic notion that birds sing because they are 'full of the joys of spring' may have little basis in fact. The prolonged singing of most species uses considerable energy and takes up valuable time, so it clearly plays an important part in the annual cycle. The defence of a territory is essential for successful breeding in most perching birds that sing. The long-distance communication provided by song is doubtless more efficient in defending territory than visible displays, especially in thick woodland. Some birds of open habitats that lack any well-developed song, such as great crested grebes, establish and defend territories using elaborate posturing and movements. However, the high flights and sustained songs of skylarks point to the advantages of singing, even in open fields.

The song of each species is different from that of all other species nesting nearby, so the communication of territorial claims does not become confused. Hence birds can be recognised from a distance and this forms the basis of a technique for counting songbirds that is widely used each year in Britain. Some of the differences between species are thought to be related to the way that sounds of different pitch can be detected in different settings, so that for example the high-pitched song of a dipper can be heard above the gurgling of streams. It is thought that the sustained nature of many birdsongs allows the singing bird to be located, a role that is often helped by its perching prominently. This contrasts markedly with alarm calls like those given when a hawk appears, which are shrill, brief and mainly given from a low perch, rendering the caller hard to see but serving to warn other birds of the predator's presence.

Studies show that individual male birds very commonly have songs that differ slightly from those of individuals singing nearby. These differences are thought to allow neighbouring territorial males to recognise each other and hence reduce unnecessary conflict, and to allow females to recognise their own mates. The beauty, richness and variety of song in some of our best songsters, such as blackbirds, emphasises the high quality of the singer as both territorial aggressor and potential father.

Soon after the male songbird establishes its territory and a mate settles in it, the pair will select a nest site and build the nest, often while continuing with courtship displays and mating. The date of laying is usually adjusted to the time when most food will be available for nestlings. Hence, many small insectivorous birds in oak woodlands hatch their young to coincide with the abundance of caterpillars in late May and early June. Finches that feed their nestlings mainly on seeds, such as linnets, tend to lay later so that their young can be reared when weed seeds are most plentiful.

OPPOSITE:
Like a blue bullet, the kingfisher flashes across the surface of the water or speeds along a river bank. Occasionally it pips a warning but usually a fleeting glimpse from the corner of a surprised eye is all that is seen. The kingfisher is a bird that excites even the hardened naturalist. Its brilliant plumage, its lightning speed and its outstanding skills as a fisherman earn it a special place in the world of birds.

Cock pheasants are conspicuously the most colourful birds of the woodlands and present a striking contrast to the drab, brown hens.

A long-eared owl listens intently for the slightest rustle in the leaves below. Then, on silent wings, the predator swoops down with pinpoint accuracy to catch an unsuspecting woodmouse or vole.

The ghostly flight of a barn owl floating on long elegant wings beside a hedgerow at dusk is now sadly a rare sight. Regarded as the emblem of British farmland, this super-efficient rodent-catcher has been in serious decline for many years. This directly reflects the often unintentional disregard that modern farming methods have for preserving certain habitats. Barn owls feed on small rodents and they in turn need rough areas of tussocky grass in which to breed. The destruction of hedgerows and old meadows has cut off food supplies, not only to barn owls, but also to many other species which are also in decline. Modern farming methods encourage large areas of monoculture and intensively managed grasslands. Neither situation offers sustainable feeding and breeding opportunities for most farmland bird species. What is required is the return of well-managed hedgerows with grassy banks on either side, linking areas of woodland together.

Thankfully, this return has started. Many farmers, foresters and conservation advisers are doing a great deal to encourage wildlife back into the countryside. The value of waterside, woodland and field margins is now recognised, as is the need to provide nesting sites. Success can only be achieved when large areas of land are managed in a similar way to create extensive networks of habitats. Success will be measured when the decline of the barn owl is reversed. That will take a well-organised effort by many people, but surely it will be worth it to see once again the ghostly flight of the white owl.

Some of the common birds such as jays and long-tailed tits raise only one brood each year, but others such as song thrushes and blackbirds often raise three and sometimes four broods in succession. Like the timing of laying, the number of broods appears to be related to the availability of suitable foods for nestlings. Both jays and long-tailed tits rely on the short-lived flush of defoliating caterpillars in woodland, so they only have the chance of a single brood. Indeed, if a pair of long-tailed tits loses a nest with eggs they often have insufficient time to start another; instead, they show most unusual behaviour for small birds in assisting a neighbouring pair to feed their nestlings. In contrast to these, blackbirds and song thrushes feed their young on a variety of insects and worms that may be available in different combinations from April until August, so they usually have time to rear several broods.

Nest-building takes several days to a week for most small birds, although the elaborate domed nest of a long-tailed tit may take as long as a month to complete and the thorny domed 'castle' of the magpies usually requires several weeks of labour. Some birds on the other hand build no nest at all or only a slight structure; the barn owl makes a mere scrape inside the nesting hollow and lapwings often amass just a few stems.

Small birds generally lay one egg a day until the clutch is complete and sustained incubation begins, but many larger birds such as barn owls lay eggs at intervals of two or even three days and these often begin incubating with the first egg. Where incubation does not start until the clutch is complete the young all hatch at about the same time, so that they remain generally similar in size. In contrast, where incubation begins with the first egg the hatching period is spread over several days and the young, being of different ages, often retain differences in size throughout the nestling period. A potential advantage of having nestlings of such differing sizes is that when food is scarce the smallest may fail to compete for food and thus die, leaving the largest chicks in good health. On the other hand, if the young are all of similar size, then all may weaken and die if food is in short supply.

The male barn owl does all the hunting for the family, and he regularly delivers rodents and passes them tenderly to his mate.

The female never leaves her chicks until they are able to feed themselves, which is usually when their new feathers start appearing through thick white down. Once this stage is reached, the female leaves the nest site for quite long periods. The male continues to deliver rodents but he is less patient than the female and so the youngsters have to help themselves. To start with, this causes great frustration and they attack the unfortunate mice by stamping on them and tossing them about while making loud hissing and gurgling noises. After much experimentation they get the idea and start to swallow a mouse whole, head first; it is more streamlined that way!

Several minutes later and after a great deal of gulping (it must be quite a challenge to swallow a dry, furry mouse, even for an owl) it throws its head back and the force of gravity takes over. Then the owlet sits there for a few moments, with eyes watering, and feeling rather uncomfortable. However, life must go on and having cracked the swallowing code the youngsters grow rapidly on a never-ending supply of rodents. The feathers of adulthood soon replace the white down of youth and the fledgling owls are ready to face the outside world where hopefully they will find suitable habitats to rear young of their own.

A woodmouse finds a morsel amongst the leaf litter.

A cock pheasant in full breeding plumage claims his territory with characteristic wing-beating and crowing.

A lizard pauses for a moment as it scuttles through a grassy patch on the edge of the moorland.

The eggs of hole-nesting birds are often white or very pale, probably so that the parent birds can see them in the gloom of the nest site and avoid accidental damage. In open nests the need for concealment from predators becomes paramount, so eggs are typically blotched, spotted or streaked to camouflage them effectively against the nest. The number of eggs laid in a clutch varies widely, from just a single egg in many seabirds to normal maxima of around fifteen in pheasants and eighteen in blue tits, with three to six being commonest in those songbirds that nest in the open. The very large clutches of pheasants and many duck species are possible because their active young receive little or no food from the parents and can be led to places with plentiful supplies soon after hatching. The very large clutches of blue tits apparently occur because the slow development of numerous eggs and nestlings is possible in a nest-hole inaccessible to predators, whereas birds that nest in the open, such as thrushes, need to complete the nesting cycle more quickly in order to minimise the high risks from predators. For the blue tit to lay such large numbers of eggs the female not only feeds actively for herself during the laying period, she also receives large amounts of food collected by her mate.

With many small birds incubation is carried out by the female bird alone, the male being occupied in the meantime with territory defence. The females of these species leave the nest at intervals to feed. With owls, and members of the crow family, the female incubates but receives much of her food at the nest from the male, an arrangement that is probably useful in ensuring that the eggs are not left untended and at risk from predators. Many larger birds such as great crested grebes and moorhens share incubation between the two sexes, with regular change-overs at the nest. The incubation period is shortest in small birds that nest in the open, taking as little as twelve to fourteen days with yellowhammers. Hole-nesters take longer, as do larger birds, especially those that have young which are well developed at hatching. The large mute swan, for example, takes around thirty-six days.

Hatching and the care of nestlings will be considered in the next section, as, for many birds, these stages are more a feature of late spring. Nevertheless, the widely differing nesting seasons of many species ensure that some early nesters such as mallard and barn owls commonly have large young before such later nesters as swallows and many finches have begun laying.

LATE SPRING

As spring continues, more and more species of plants come into flower. The main exception is on the woodland floor, which becomes shaded as the tree canopy develops. It is true that late spring and early summer see the appearance of some very spectacular shade-tolerating flowers on the woodland floor, including some of the orchids, but these are much scarcer and less obvious than the primroses and bluebells which flower before the shady canopy develops. The high canopies of the woodland trees are of course less shaded and there such species as the two oaks and beech flower as they come into leaf during the spring, but their wind-pollinated flowers are green and inconspicuous.

The edges of woodland are also less shaded. For this reason they are often rich in shrubs that flower in late spring, typically including hawthorn, dog rose, woody nightshade and elder; the latter does not flower until the very end of spring. Many others may occur where soils are suitable for them, including dogwood, privet, buckthorn and spindle-tree on limey soils, and guelder rose and alder buckthorn on the wetter soils. Hedgerows also provide good habitats for many of these shrubs, especially the oldest hedges such as those beside old tracks. Indeed, it has been found that the approximate age of a hedgerow can be gauged from the total number of shrub species it contains.

In farmland the hedgerows and the adjacent strips of field edge provide the most important habitat available to many plants and animals. The economies needed for modern farming practice have resulted in the destruction of hedgerows in many parts of the country and many of the remaining hedges are in a poor state as traditional labour-intensive hedge management has declined or disappeared. Fortunately, landowners who are interested in wildlife conservation can recreate the rich diversity of old hedges quite easily in a new hedge by planting an appropriate diversity of young shrubs. Such efforts begin to show rewards within a few years as a wide variety of butterflies and nesting birds colonise the hedge; visiting birds will feast on the berries of its shrubs in winter.

The wild flowers of cultivated fields are much more difficult to protect. Fifty years ago arable fields supported a rich variety of weeds that often included such attractive wild flowers as corn-cockle and corn buttercup, as well as the more familiar corn poppy. The development of modern techniques for cleaning crop seeds has resulted in a great reduction in the quantity and variety of weed seed accidentally sown with crops, while the application of selective herbicides ensures that few of the weeds that do arrive and germinate ever grow to set seed. As a result of these changes many of the weeds of arable fields have become rare in Britain. Of course, farmers cannot be expected to revert to less efficient methods of crop production and consumers would anyway no longer tolerate grain that is heavily contaminated with weed seeds. The main hope then for the long-term survival of some of the rarest weeds lies in their being tolerated on small areas at the margins of certain fields, where they are not sprayed with the weedkillers used elsewhere. It is to be hoped that such efforts will suffice to prevent the extinction in the wild of some of these plants, as has already happened in Britain to interrupted brome-grass and flax dodder.

Small ponds were also once a traditional feature of many farmland regions. Most of them were originally dug out to provide water for cattle and other farm stock, although the larger ones sometimes served as fish ponds. They were quickly colonised by a wide variety of aquatic and marginal plants, as well as by frogs, newts, dragonflies and moorhens. The modern husbandry of farm animals has led to many of the ponds being replaced by more reliable supplies of cleaner water, so that few of them are

OPPOSITE:
Beautiful meadow saxifrage grows in unimproved grassland.

Moonwort, a strange fern which grows in short turf.

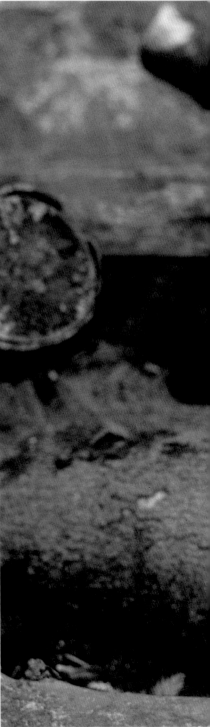

A fox cub playing on an old wood pile. Vulpes vulpes *is a handsome and cunning survivor. I always feel a buzz of excitement when I spot one loping across a field or darting across a woodland ride. They are of course ruthless killers of wildlife and poultry, and in some areas they kill young lambs and piglets. For this reason their numbers have to be controlled and this is most effectively done by the people who monitor fox populations and their predatory activities.*

left in most regions and those that survive are often choked with dumped rubbish and overgrown vegetation. The loss of so many ponds has led to drastic declines in some of their typical plants and animals, one of those to have suffered badly being the great crested newt. Seasonal ponds, which dry in a good summer, also support a characteristic range of plants and animals including starfruit, which has now become very rare.

Fortunately, ponds are easy to recreate and many of their characteristic plants and animals soon arrive of their own accord. Care should be taken if plants or animals are deliberately introduced to a new pond, since many of those favoured by aquarists and found in garden ponds are not native to Britain and are prone to increase rapidly at the expense of our natives. The invasive aliens include a number of aggressively successful waterweeds, such as Canadian pondweed, New Zealand pigmyweed and curly waterweed, which are now showing signs of spreading across Britain without human aid. With a few exceptions, exotic animals are less conspicuously successful in British ponds, although there are fears that red-necked terrapins and American bullfrogs liberated in recent years may become established and damage native fauna. American mink which became established in the wild after escaping from fur farms have now increased greatly in numbers and spread along rivers and streams over much of Britain. They are thought to be at least partly to blame for the great decline of our native water vole and there are fears that their increasing numbers may adversely affect otter populations.

Wet and marshy fields are another type of wildlife habitat that has declined greatly in many farmland areas. Improved land drainage has allowed farmers to bring many of these fields into more productive use, but attractive plants such as marsh orchids and ragged robin are then lost. Protecting some of the best of the surviving marshy areas, even in nature reserves, is often problematical because they tend to dry out as the water table is lowered on surrounding land.

Another problem affecting wildlife in marshes, ponds, streams and rivers alike is the tendency for nutrient enrichment to occur through the run-off of nitrates and phosphates from agricultural land. In some streams and rivers this problem is worsened by the discharge of sewage. The characteristic plants of many marshy or aquatic habitats are those that are associated with low natural levels of nutrients. If the levels of nutrients are increased the composition of the vegetation usually changes, because species able to use the higher nutrient levels increase at the expense of those which cannot. The long-stalked pondweed has become rare in southern England because of such nutrient enrichment of its waters, and numerous other species have also suffered. On the other hand, the pollution-tolerant fennel pondweed has probably increased. Many of these effects are difficult to reduce, although the control of inputs of sewage and some other nutrient sources are the responsibility of the river and water authorities.

The short turf on chalk and limestone slopes is rich with wild flowers in late spring and summer. These may include relatively common plants such as milkwort, yellow rattle, ox-eye daisy, wild thyme and birds-foot trefoil, scarcer ones such as pyramidal orchid and bee orchid, and localised rarities like perennial flax. Taller grassland over the same limey soils is less rich in species, but often has field scabious among its specialities and the rare fly orchid may occur at the edge of the scrub. Botanists continue to argue about the reasons why grasslands on limey soil support such a rich variety of plants, although it is clear that the short open turf is important to the survival of many of them. When grazing pressure declines, taller grasses take over and many of the smaller plants are lost. Further neglect may lead to colonisation by scrub and saplings, and most of the special grassland plants have by then been lost.

OPPOSITE:
Canada geese are large and noisy birds. They are not native to Britain, but are now well established, with flocks in areas where there are good stretches of fresh water. They are extremely aggressive parents, protecting their goslings against all comers including foxes. As a result numbers are growing rapidly in many areas, sometimes causing damage to waterside habitats and farmland.

Tufted ducks, affectionately known as 'tufties', disperse from large wintering flocks to breed in pairs on small lakes and ponds. They start courtship later than other ducks, during April. The brown female lays a clutch of creamy eggs which she conceals in a snug nest in thick vegetation only a few feet from the water's edge. It is our most common diving duck and depends on high-quality, unpolluted water for its food supply of freshwater molluscs, shrimps, small fish and water plants.

Orchids are particularly plentiful in the better chalk and limestone grasslands, with more species than in other habitats and often many individual plants. Although less showy than the tropical orchids, our fifty or so native species are a strange and varied group of plants that have always held a special fascination for naturalists. Their seeds are extremely tiny and probably disperse by blowing on the wind. To become established their root systems need to be intricately associated with special mycorrhizal fungi. Individual plants of some of the species do not flower until they are five years or more old and mature plants may not produce any leaves or stems one year, then unexpectedly reappear above ground the next. Their elaborately shaped flowers are adapted for pollination by a variety of insects, which leave with stalked bags of pollen (pollinia) attached to their heads or bodies, rather than the fine dust of pollen presented by most flowers. Flowers on the bee and fly orchids mimic solitary bees, males of which misguidedly make repeated attempts to mate with the flowers and hence cause pollination. Added to all these peculiarities, some of our native orchids are both beautiful and extremely rare, so it is not surprising that devotees travel long distances to see and photograph them.

Calcareous grasslands are also noteworthy for the richness of their butterflies. Some species such as the small blue, adonis blue and marbled white are mostly confined to these habitats, while many others that are wider ranging also occur there. The distribution of favoured food plants such as the lime-loving horseshoe vetch and kidney vetch accounts for the occurrence of many of these butterflies on chalky soils. Some of the blues also need ants, which tend and protect their caterpillars in return for secretions from the larval honey-gland which they eat. The preference of marbled whites for chalky soils is harder to explain, however, since their larvae feed on several common and widespread species of grasses.

A green hairstreak resting on spurge. These attractive little butterflies are found on heathland where their caterpillars feed on gorse and broom.

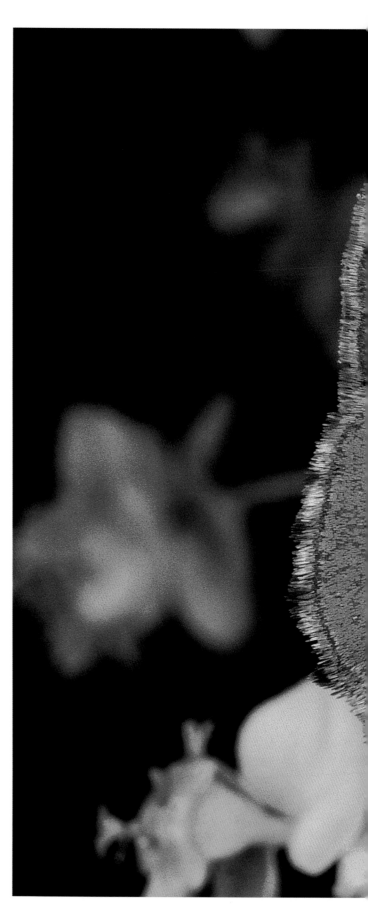

Milkwort, a very common, small plant that grows close to the ground on moorland, dunes and limestone. It is so insignif-icant that it usually goes unnoticed, but this close-up taken on Jura picks out the attractive flowers.

A magnificent golden-ringed dragonfly perches on bog myrtle as the early morning sun energises its torpid body to give it the power of flight.

The greater butterfly orchid is a rare and graceful plant growing in woodland glades and unimproved grassland. This specimen was standing alone and supreme amongst a group of common spotted orchids. I photographed it in a heavy drizzle just as the sky had lightened a little.

A fine group of common spotted orchids growing in typical unimproved grassland, with sedges and quaking grass offering little competition for space.

A male redstart carries a beak full of insects to feed his hungry chicks, well concealed in a cavity high up in an oak tree. This colourful bird is very secretive when brooding eggs but is very obvious when feeding fledglings. Their flashing rusty-coloured tails and continuous anxious calling quickly draw attention to their presence.

Wild dog roses add beauty to hedgerows. Later in the year the red hips provide winter feeding for birds, woodmice and voles.

Thick hedgerows provide ideal nesting cover for green-finches. Wide grassy field margins growing between the crops and the hedgerows provide areas where wild flowers can support large numbers of insects. The seeds of the plants are a valuable food source for several species of finches.

A parent little owl has just delivered an earthworm to this fledgling who is not quite sure how to handle the wriggling monster.

A young nightjar, incredibly well camouflaged on the woodland floor. Watching these strange birds displaying over their breeding territories at dusk is an unforgettable experience. Forestry methods of clear-felling and replanting provide ideal habitats for these exciting birds. They like young fir plantations, over which they can hunt for moths at night. As the young trees grow to meet each other the birds move on to colonise a younger stand of trees, where they can nest in between them.

A common darter uses unfurling bracken as a launching pad to hunt for passing flies.

Tawny owls are very successful colonisers, adapting to varied habitats and feeding on a wide variety of prey. This bird, still with the down of youth clinging to new feathers, looks alert with its large, light-gathering eyes.

A busy blue tit makes dozens of feeding trips every day,
carrying insects and caterpillars to a hungry brood of chicks.

A female goldfinch begs for food from her mate as she broods their chicks. It is a delight to watch charms of goldfinches feeding on groundsel and thistle seeds. The birds move from plant to plant with a dancing flight accompanied by tinkling calls.

A burst of thistle down.

A female sparrowhawk feeds her nearly full-grown chicks on the remains of a wood pigeon caught by her mate.

Foxgloves grow on dry, acid soils and usually colonise disturbed ground in woodlands, often creating spectacular stands of brilliant red fairy thimbles.

*Frog orchids are probably more common than people realise;
they are very difficult to find, growing in unimproved grassland.*

The fly orchid is a rather rare plant which grows on chalky soils along woodland margins and in rocky places.

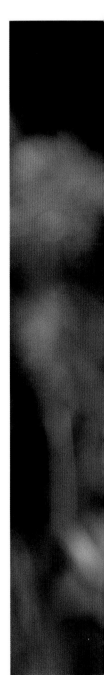

A wall butterfly feeding on common knapweed. This species benefits from wide field margins where grasses such as cocksfoot grow to feed its caterpillars.

A close-up shot of a bee orchid flower highlights a pollen sac which is ready to be brushed off onto the back of a visiting bee. This superb orchid grows on impoverished chalky soils and like many plants relies on the sensitive management of grazing livestock.

*Corncockle was once a common plant growing in cornfields
but is now rare. The black, poisonous seeds contaminated
the crops and the plant was therefore eradicated from fields
but this annual can still be found on field margins.*

*Birdsfoot trefoil has bright little flowers. It grows on dry
grassy places and its leaves are eaten by the caterpillars of
the common blue butterfly.*

A leveret makes the most of a sunny bank. Hares are at home on farmland, where they sit nearly out of sight in their forms during the day. As evening falls they become more active as they start to feed; they particularly like sweet young grass. During the mating season in early spring they can often be seen skipping after each other across fields, stopping now and again for a stand-up boxing match.

The tall and elegant stems of field scabious carry a cushion of tiny individual flowers. The plant thrives on unimproved chalk grassland where it attracts many species of butterflies, feeding on the nectar.

The beautiful perennial flax is a rare plant growing on chalky soils where sensitive grazing techniques are applied.

A female bullfinch broods her newly hatched chicks. This striking finch is easily recognised by its black cap, conspicuous white rump and the male's scarlet breast. The species is attracted to large hedgerows and thickets of hawthorn and blackthorn. Its presence is marked by soft piping calls repeated at intervals.

Numerous butterfly species of other habitats also emerge in late spring. Small pearl-bordered fritillaries appear in woodland clearings and along rides where dog violet, the larval food plant, grows. The wall butterfly appears in a variety of sunny spots, such as along garden paths, in old quarries and on banks, but considering that its larvae feed on the commonest of grasses it is strangely uncommon and localised. The numbers and diversity of moths increase as spring continues, with such spectacular species as the elephant hawk-moth emerging, but the greatest diversity of moths is really reserved for mid and late summer. Early dragonflies and damselflies appear in numbers in late spring, especially near the ponds, streams and rivers where their larval and pupal stages are spent underwater.

The early spring tadpoles of frogs and toads have metamorphosed into tiny 'froglets' and 'toadlets' that are miniature replicas of the adults. These make their way into land to begin the terrestrial life of the adults. Grass snakes feed avidly on the 'froglets' while they are in or near the water, but their numbers are so vast that the snakes, and bird predators such as herons, only make a dent in the population.

Late spring is also an active time for many animals. The new flush of plant growth allows breeding to recommence in mice, voles, rabbits and brown hares, while increased insect abundance allows breeding by shrews, hedgehogs and bats. Young foxes grow rapidly and emerge from cover to take advantage of the rich pickings of prey such as voles, young rabbits and young birds, learning how to catch these at a time of plenty.

Just before sunset one evening I found this superb marbled white butterfly roosting on a lesser knapweed bud. As the light faded, the evening breeze subsided and I managed to approach to within only a few inches. My photographs taken, I left him to spend the night safe on his knapweed tower.

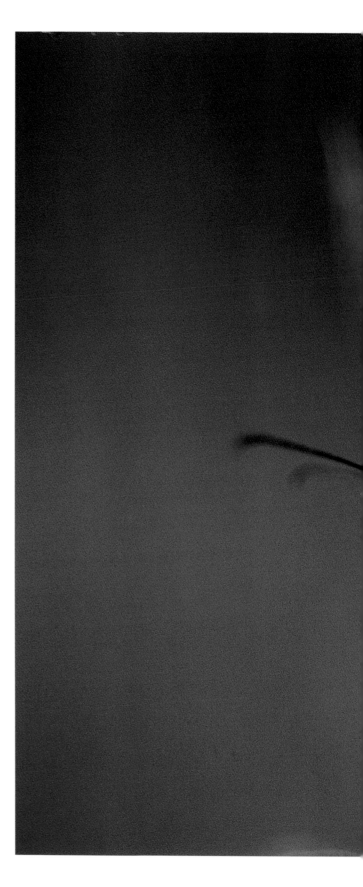

I spent many hours in a hide watching and photographing both birds as they carried food to their youngsters. The hole in the tree faced north so, to make the most of natural light, I visited the hide early in the morning and during the evenings. Those are also the best times to watch other birds going about their busy lives, like the great spotted wood-peckers feeding their noisy chicks just 30 yards away.

After about four weeks, the young greens started popping their heads out of their hole, clamouring for 'insect soup' regurgitated by their parents. One evening, a week or so later, I was in my hide when the male bird seemed to be concerned that the young ones were becoming too large and outgrowing the size of the exit! This prompted immediate action and he decided it was fledging time. But to extricate the youngsters from their wooden home proved to be a noisy and stressful process. To my amazement, he tempted the first one out with insect soup and encouraged it with vocal sounds. Gradually, the fledgling wriggled free. When it first

appeared, I was surprised by how pale its feathers were. Then suddenly, the brand-new woodpecker saw the 40 foot drop to the woodland floor and started clinging on for dear life. It then panicked and tried to get back into the safety of the hole, but its nest mates prevented it, attacking it with hammering beaks.

By this time, all the squeaking and squawking had attracted the attention of the female and she arrived on the scene to join in with the chorus of anxiety. The beleaguered youngster realised that its only escape was upwards. It resorted to instinct, clapped its stiff little tail to the tree trunk and hauled itself up on wobbly legs. I was mesmerised. The other three chicks left the nest in a similar fashion. When the last one had climbed successfully up the tree all went quiet. I sat in my hide for a while feeling quite exhausted. I then realised that I had witnessed a very special event, and one which I will probably never see again.

*Little owls are comical characters. During the day they can
sometimes be seen near farmland, perching on fencing posts
paying close attention to the surrounding area.*

Or utter surprise may follow the whirring of a black beetle as
it flies close by.

Or maybe the hunter will be mesmerised by the leisurely flight
of a moth dancing across the shadows.

For many people, the badger is their favourite British mammal. Persecuted over the years, it now enjoys legal protection and numbers are expanding as a result. However, the incredibly cruel sport of badger-baiting still goes on. In some areas the animals are in conflict with cattle farmers, who blame them for spreading tuberculosis to dairy herds.

I designed this pond to blend in with the surrounding land-scape and to enhance the visual appeal of the valley. From a conservation point of view, the aim of the project was to create varied habitats. For instance, by providing an island water birds are able to nest safely. The margins surrounding the pond were fenced off to safeguard plants and grasses and the depth of the pond was made variable to support both dabbling and diving ducks. It has been a delight to watch the project mature. The plants are flourishing, several bird species rear their young here and an osprey has called in to catch a fish or two.

Well-managed marshy margins surrounding ponds and waterways provide excellent habitats for many forms of wildlife. Thick areas of soft rush are ideal for birds such as the reed bunting to nest in.

The untidy flowers of ragged robin add a splash of colour to the rush beds and attract many insects to feed on nectar.

Handsome marsh orchids are quite common and can grow up to 2 feet high. I once found one with a flower-head 9 inches tall.

All is not well for this reed warbler. Her nest has been hijacked by a cuckoo and she now has her work cut out feeding a forever hungry monster. Earlier the newly hatched cuckoo chick ejected the eggs of the unfortunate warbler from the nest. For many people the calls of the cuckoo are a sure sign that summer is just around the corner. But the sound is not as common as it used to be because like many other species it is in decline due to loss of habitat.

A fledgling cuckoo soon outgrows the fragile nest of a reed warbler.

An elephant hawk-moth feeding on honeysuckle.

As the elephant hawk-moth moves through the honeysuckle *petals feeding on nectar, pollen grains are dusted onto its furry forehead where they are ready to pollinate the next flower it visits.*

Migration of one bird species or another continues from late winter throughout spring into early summer. Birds that are only winter visitors to most of Britain such as redwings and fieldfares gradually decline in numbers until all have left. The emigration of the hordes of starlings, chaffinches, blackbirds and song thrushes that visit Britain for the winter is even less noticeable, since our resident populations of these species remain with us. Geese, ducks and waders leave our estuaries for their northern breeding grounds, but the departure of some of these is masked as birds that have wintered further south pass through Britain as spring migrants. By late spring, however, most have gone and the few flocks of waders on our estuaries are more likely to consist of birds travelling between Africa and the Arctic than those that spent the winter here.

The arrival of summer visitors is much more conspicuous than the departure of wintering birds. The first sand-martins and wheatears usually arrive in southern England in March, the first swallows a short time after, while swifts typically do not appear until the beginning of May and nightjars may be still later. In between, redstarts, many warblers, flycatchers and a host of others make their appearance. In general, it would appear that each species times its return to coincide with the occurrence of a reliable supply of food. For most of the summer visitors this is insect food and those species relying on an abundance of large flying insects, such as spotted flycatchers and nightjars, are among the latest to return. Some of these spring migrants are just passing through Britain, bound for more northerly breeding grounds like those of the Greenland and Iceland populations of wheatears. Others are returning to breeding grounds here.

Extending the width of field margins between crops and hedgerows or woodlands has major benefits for wildlife populations. In fact, I believe that well-managed margins rich in wild flowers and grasses are just as important as the hedgerows themselves. The plants attract butterflies and insects, and their seeds provide vital feeding resources for voles and many bird species. I have developed an effective method of establishing field margins by drilling the seeds of grasses such as cocksfoot timothy and fescues in a strip about 6 feet wide at the edge of the field. The best sites are usually

south or west-facing where there are signs of indigenous wild flowers although they can be introduced by including their seeds in the grass mixture.

With most of the small summer visitors, such as redstarts and reed warblers, most males arrive a few days ahead of most females. Old males tend to arrive before younger ones. The majority of these returning birds travel directly to their breeding grounds, which are typically where they have nested before or near to where they themselves were reared. The returning males almost immediately begin to sing and defend territories, so that by the time the females arrive they are in a good position to attract a mate and commence nesting. With most of these smaller migrants a new mate is found each year, although if the mate of the previous year returns the same pair may be re-established.

The numbers of migrants returning each year can vary considerably. For whitethroats and sandmartins it is now known that the conditions on the wintering grounds in the Sahel region along the southern edge of the Sahara are important. When the monsoon rains in the Sahel are deficient fewer birds survive the winter, so fewer return to breed in Britain. Of course, these species also rely

The flowers of woody nightshade growing in a hedgerow.

on the presence of suitable nesting habitats and the whitethroat has undoubtedly declined in some areas because of the loss of hedgerows.

By the time most of the summer migrants have returned and established their territories many of our resident birds are well advanced with nesting and some, such as robins and blackbirds, may already be attending their second broods. The nestlings of most of these small birds are fed by both parents, but for at least the first few days one parent needs to brood the young to keep them warm. As they grow larger and feathers develop there is less need for brooding, so that both parents can concentrate on satisfying their increasing demands for food. Small birds may carry food to the nest as often as ten times an hour throughout the day, a schedule so demanding that other activities such as singing and territory defence are much reduced and the parent birds lose weight. The young of most small

birds fledge after ten to fifteen days in the nest, but receive food from their parents for at least a few days afterwards. Fortunately for the parents, the fledged young can often be moved closer to food sources so that the strain of feeding the family can be reduced.

Predators such as sparrowhawks and owls catch larger and more nutritious food than the small insectivorous birds like warblers, but their prey is much more difficult and time-consuming to obtain. Hence they feed their young less often than do small birds, but give them larger meals. Their longer fledging periods and more prolonged periods of post-fledging care allow them to rear only a single brood each year. A special problem for owls is that whereas most birds benefit from the longer days when they are feeding young, the shorter nights give owls less hunting time than was available earlier in the year. Some owls, especially the little owl, reduce this problem by doing some of their hunting in daylight when the demands of feeding the young are greatest.

The small pearl-bordered fritillary is widespread and can be found in woodland margins and heathland where its caterpillars feed on violets.

By laying in the nests of other birds the female cuckoo avoids caring for its own young, enabling it to produce more offspring. Although it might be thought that this gives cuckoos a lazy way of life, the reality is that the female cuckoo must spend a great deal of time and energy finding the nests of hosts that are at the laying stage in order to lay each of her own eggs at the appropriate time. The success of nest parasitism by cuckoos is presumably evidence that host species such as reed warblers have very strong instincts to feed young birds in their nests and little or no ability to discriminate between their own young and the much larger young cuckoos. Another peculiar feature of cuckoos is that the young bird never sees its true parents, so that when it becomes adult its choice of mate must be based only on instinct.

A fledgling kestrel welcomes the arrival of a parent bird as it flies in with another vole. Kestrels regularly hunt field margins and other rough areas of grass.

They also readily take up the offer of artificial nesting boxes, provided that they are sited close to good hunting areas.

A brood of young swallows sing for their supper.

MOORLANDS, MOUNTAINS AND NORTHERN COASTS

Spring arrives late in the uplands of Britain and the far north. The short growing season ensures that few crops can be grown and the predominance of poor acidic soils only reinforces these limitations. Large areas of moorland and mountain slopes are grazed, especially by sheep, but others are so poor and cold that they are left to the grouse, deer and other wildlife. The higher mountain slopes, especially those facing north, may retain patches of snow into summer, so that only specialised plants able to tolerate a very short growing season can survive there.

To understand these wild and beautiful places and their wildlife it is helpful to know something of the history that has shaped them. Of greatest importance is the legacy from a succession of geological stages with very cold climates, the last of which ended around 10,000 years ago. During parts of these cold stages most of the British mountains were buried beneath thick ice-caps, with glaciers occupying the valleys. The ice stripped away rock to produce the Scottish corries (Welsh cwms) and other landforms, removing older soils from the slopes and valleys. When the ice was at its maximum there would have been little scope for plant and animal life in the mountains. However, fossil records show that the cold lowlands of that time supported what are now mountain plants and animals, as shown for example by leaves of mountain avens and bones of ptarmigan found in river deposits near London.

After most of the mountain ice thawed with the rapid climatic warming around 10,000 years ago the cold-tolerant plants and animals re-

colonised the mountains. Woodlands of birch, then pine, then oaks became established in the lowlands and the cold-tolerant, open country plants and animals became restricted to the newly reoccupied high ground.

By around 7,000 years ago the forests that covered much of Britain extended higher onto the mountain slopes than they do now, covering for example much of the present-day moorlands of the Pennines. Since then the altitudinal tree-line has been considerably lowered. A slight cooling in the climate has been partly responsible for this lowering, but the destruction of forest by early human pastoralists followed by a deterioration in the soils was probably more important. At the present day a combination of impoverished soils and heavy grazing prevents woodlands from attaining their former altitudinal limits. In some areas, trees growing on inaccessible rock ledges on otherwise treeless mountain slopes provide a clear demonstration of what the vegetation might be like if the grazing pressure were to be reduced.

This history accounts for the patterns of distribution of our mountain plants and animals. The beautiful mountain avens now occupies widely scattered localities in the mountains of northern England and Scotland, with one in north Wales, but descends to near sea level in parts of the far north of Scotland and in western Ireland, as it does in the Arctic. In southern Europe it occurs only at high elevations in the mountains. The fossil records of this species from the lowlands show clearly that its present-day scatter of widely separated localities is a relict from a much more continuous distribution when the climate was colder.

Mountain plants requiring limestone soils are especially restricted because so much of the British uplands consist of acid siliceous rocks. For example, the splendid spring gentian is a rarity confined in the British Isles to limestone mountains in northern England and small areas on lower ground on the west coast of Ireland. The wider distribution of this species includes the mountains of central and southern Europe, Arctic Russia and northern Asia, so it too can probably be regarded as showing a relict distribution from a colder climatic stage.

Grazing pressure from sheep has affected the vegetation on large areas of our mountains. Poor grasslands dominated by mat grass now occupy large areas of the Welsh mountains, with richer vegetation that includes many of the special mountain plants restricted to inaccessible ledges. Grazing by deer has had similar effects in the Scottish mountains, where such showy plants as blue sow-thistle occur only on ungrazed rock ledges. Nevertheless, such grazing pressure has existed for many years and the flora has attained an equilibrium with it. Overall, threats to the mountain plants are fortunately few compared to those in many lowland habitats, so long as unscrupulous collecting is avoided and careful controls are placed on developments such as those for ski-lifts in the Cairngorms.

Only fragments of the original woodlands now remain in our mountain areas. Among the most precious of these are the native Scots pine forests of Strathspey and a few other parts of Scotland, and smaller areas of birch woodland elsewhere in the Scottish mountains. These remnants of boreal forest support animals and plants that have very restricted ranges in Britain but which are commoner in Scandinavia, where extensive boreal forests remain. Their floras include the delicate chickweed wintergreen (despite its name, a member of the primrose family) and the round-leaved wintergreen. The faunas include pine marten, wildcat and the splendid, turkey-sized capercaillie. The Scottish native pine forests are also the home of two birds found nowhere else in the world, although they show only rather subtle differences from European relatives: the Scottish subspecies of the crested tit and the Scottish crossbill.

The Paps of Jura. Over remote hills and mountains, beautiful, wild landscapes unfold. Many of our rarest birds, animals and plants inhabit these forbidding places. So unique are such habitats that they must be preserved and safeguarded from the destructive forces of commercial gain.

114

Many ancient herds of wild goats roam in remote mountain and island locations. Their long shaggy coats keep them warm in the winter and the huge horns of the males are used as weapons of war when battles for females take place.

The very rare dwarf cornel growing on high heather moorland. It grows in large clumps, and the first sight of its beautiful flowers is enough to take one's breath away. I took this photograph shortly after sunrise on the North York Moors one morning in May. The first rays of the sun delicately glance off the drying leaves and flowers.

Although spring gentian is common in Europe, it only grows here high in Teesdale. Once seen, the incredible blueness of this superb flower will never be forgotten.

A moorland stream flows gently over boulders. On the banks, bilberry, heather and bog-myrtle grow between the alder and silver birch trees. This is a habitat which supports an ecosystem all of its own, and which enjoys protection in many national nature reserves and parks.

*High on heather moorland a cock grouse struts across his
territory.*

The delicate hoary rock-rose is a rare plant growing on limestone in Wales and northern England.

Mountain avens is a rare and distinctive arctic-alpine plant. It grows on limestone mountains in Wales, northern England and Scotland.

Britain's largest woodland bird, the capercaillie, establishes his nesting territory in the magnificent pine forests of Scotland.

Mountain everlasting is a plant that grows in upland pastures in the north.

Large areas of hill country and the lower mountain slopes are covered by heather and other low shrubs, forming moorland vegetation that is similar in many respects to lowland heaths. Most moorland owes its origins to ancient deforestation, but many areas have long been managed for red grouse shooting. The management normally involves periodic burning, which destroys tall old heather and encourages new growth. It also tends to encourage the heather to dominate other plants. Some heather moors still support the beautiful dwarf cornel, which was originally a plant of heathy boreal forests and has survived in these areas since they were deforested.

Wet bogs overlying accumulated peat and dominated by a squelchy carpet of sphagnum mosses occupy much of the low ground in hill and moorland regions. They are poor in nutrients and support a distinctive range of plants that includes the insectivorous sundews and butterwort. Edges of bogs often have such spectacular orchids as the heath spotted orchid and northern marsh orchid, and sometimes also marsh helleborine, among a wide variety of other flowers that commonly includes lousewort. Only the deepest and wettest bogs are dangerous places, but the interested naturalist should remember that bog surfaces have a fragile vegetation cover that is easily damaged by trampling and that the waders nesting on many bogs are susceptible to disturbance.

Moorland and mountain areas are the haunts of a spectacular range of predatory birds, which may include the golden eagle, hen harrier, peregrine and merlin, as well as the commoner buzzard, sparrowhawk and kestrel.

Sharp eyesight and a powerful beak equips the buzzard to hunt its prey.

Dramatic declines in the populations of two of the most spectacular raptors occurred during the 1960s and 1970s. Fortunately, research workers identified the causes and steps were taken to eradicate them, so that both have now attained something like their former numbers. For the peregrine the cause of decline was found to be persistent residues of organo-chlorine insecticides, especially DDT and its derivatives. These chemicals were eaten by pigeons and other prey taken by the peregrines, then accumulated in their fatty tissues, resulting eventually in the thinning of eggshells so that they broke their own eggs and failed to rear young. Golden eagles suffered similar problems, but obtained the DDT residues by eating the carrion of sheep that had been through chemical dips incorporating DDT. A successful voluntary ban on the use of DDT removed the cause of these problems, but only after large declines had occurred in populations of both peregrines and golden eagles. These examples should perhaps warn us of the complexity of natural environments and the subtle and invidious effects that chemical contaminants can have on them.

The sea cliffs of northern and western Britain provide some of the richest wildlife habitats in Europe as well as some of the finest scenery. Frequent drenching with salt spray prevents most plants from growing in exposed coastal sites, but a special flora of salt-tolerant plants gives them a distinctive vegetation different to anything occurring inland. In early spring the white flowers of common scurvy-grass brighten the scene, while blue-flowered spring squill sometimes forms large patches in short turf. Soon afterwards many cliff slopes have masses of the pink heads of thrift (often known as sea-pink) or sheets of the white-flowered sea-campion. Other cliff plants flower much later, not until well into summer in the case of rock samphire and rock sea-lavender.

On a distant beach at dawn the spray skips on the breakers. The surf rolls in to kiss the shore as the pale sun melts the mist. Grey turns to blue and bronze as sea and hills warm for an instant to the new day's light.

Black guillemots rest on the Holm O Papa. In the distance the windswept maritime heathland of Papa Westray supports fascinating plant and bird colonies which are adapted to an incredibly inhospitable environment.

The gannet's 6-foot wing span, spectacular diving techniques and social behaviour make it our most impressive sea
bird. It nests in huge, noisy and smelly colonies and once
paired the birds nurture a close relationship which is contin-
ually bonded by greeting rituals and preening.

A heath spotted orchid growing in short vegetation. This tiny plant survives in harsh, windy conditions by keeping its head down.

Arctic skua chicks are well camouflaged as they 'freeze'
amongst the sparse vegetation on maritime moorland.

Lousewort is a common plant that grows close to the ground
on acid heathlands.

The almost iridescent flower of the northern marsh orchid seems out of place in the otherwise drab marshy depressions on moorland.

An eider duck incubates her eggs in heavy drizzle blown by a cold northerly wind. A true sea duck, she usually nests on maritime heathland or on islands where she incubates her eggs over long unbroken periods for a month. I once found twenty-three nests built in a long line amongst the debris which had been tossed high up the beach by a winter storm.

*Most people regard puffins as their favourite sea-birds. Their
colourful bills, their sorrowful eyes and the way they waddle
about on the land endears this colourful bird to the hearts of
many.*

The cliffs of Marwich Head on the mainland of Orkney attract large numbers of nesting sea-birds.

Nesting sea-birds perhaps provide the greatest spectacle of these rocky coasts, especially where there are large cliffs or undisturbed islets. By late spring narrow cliff ledges may be covered by thousands of nesting guillemots and kittiwakes. Wider ledges may have fulmars, shags and herring gulls. Steep grassy slopes often have more colonies of gulls and in favoured places they are riddled with thousands of burrows of nesting puffins. Slopes with boulders providing safe crevices are chosen by razorbills and black guillemots.

Islets on which there is only minimal disturbance commonly have many nesting herring gulls and lesser black-backed gulls, some have colonies of cormorants and great black-backed gulls, and a few are the traditional sites of gannet colonies. Other sea-birds have different preferences for their nest sites. The arctic tern nests in colonies at the head of rocky or sandy beaches. Arctic skuas and great skuas have more widely spaced nests on moorland near the coast, often on islands.

There is clearly intense competition for nesting sites on many of the coastal cliffs, where it is commonplace to see birds fighting for possession of a favoured ledge. Space on islets may also be scarce, so that cormorants and gannets nest in dense colonies, where each pair vigorously defends its site. All of these birds need nesting places where they are safe from predation by stoats, foxes and man. Since their colonies are so conspicuous they can only achieve this safety by selecting inaccessible places in which to nest.

Although its nesting burrows are less conspicuous, the small puffin also needs to be safe from bigger birds, particularly the predatory great black-backed gull. It finds this safety by nesting underground, a strategy adopted in less extreme form also by the cavity-nesting razorbill and black guillemot.

Other coastal birds such as the oystercatcher have widely spaced nests and camouflaged eggs and chicks, so that they rely on a combination of the camouflage and cautious parental behaviour for safety from predators. Skuas and arctic terns are too conspicuous to rely just on the camouflage of their eggs and chicks. Instead they vigorously attack any potential predator that approaches their offspring, swooping low and pecking violently. When attacking people they often draw blood with their beaks and their apparent ferocity makes a lasting impression on a dog, so there is little doubt that they are also effective against natural predators such as foxes.

The persistent presence of thieving gulls around sea-bird colonies, and the loitering crows and jackdaws, mean that such sea-birds as guillemots and kittiwakes must maintain a constant vigil at nest sites with eggs or small chicks. Birdwatchers should always remember that if they approach so closely as to disturb the parent birds they risk allowing these predators to steal the nest contents.

The loss of eggs or chicks is much more serious for many sea-birds than for small birds. All of them have a single brood each year, and many, such as guillemots and fulmars, lay only a single egg. Fulmars do not relay that year if the egg is lost, while guillemots only relay if it is lost in the early part of the breeding season. Furthermore, most sea-birds do not breed until they are several years old, five on average for guillemots and nine for fulmars.

The need for one parent to guard the nest site while the other travels long distances at sea to find food accounts for the single egg of many sea-birds; it would be impossible to feed a second chick. The need to develop hunting skills before nesting doubtless accounts for the deferment of maturity for so many years. Such low productivity is only possible because adult sea-birds are normally very long lived. Studies of birds marked with rings reveal that fulmars can live to over forty years old and once past the risky juvenile stage, a gannet has an average life expectancy of sixteen years. These ages are far in excess of those of small birds: a blackbird which lived to be five years old would be unusually lucky.

A cormorant pants in the heat of the midday sun.

A young heron is ready to take off from the cliff where it was reared.

A kittiwake protects her chick from the cold drizzle blowing across the cliff.

A family of thirteen shelduck ducklings are closely shepherded by their parents as they feed near the tide line on Jura.

The subtle colours of a shag are highlighted against the blue sea.

An arctic tern hovers before diving into the sea to catch sand eels. These graceful but noisy birds protect their colonies by launching aggressive attacks on unwelcome intruders such as foxes and humans.

The velvet head of a razorbill.

The rare marsh helleborine has exquisite flowers. This superb orchid tends to grow in large numbers where it is found on fens and dune slacks.

The burning wreck of Papa Westray. An old wooden fishing boat lies useless on its side above the high water mark, its working days long since gone. On the shoreline the gulls flock noisily and a small group of dunlin hang on the wind for a fleeting moment before alighting near the water's edge. Another glorious day is drawing to a close as the sun sinks slowly towards the silhouette. As a dark cloud passes over, the sun bursts through a hole in the ancient timbers and for a moment the old wreck is no longer useless.

Under natural circumstances the slow population turnover of long-lived sea-birds need be no handicap to them, as witness the large number of sea-bird species occurring over most of the world's oceans. However, they are very poorly adapted to withstanding any unnatural mortality of adult birds. The effect of excessive hunting is apparent from the history of the great auk, which became extinct in 1844; this giant flightless relative of the razorbill formerly bred on offshore islets from Scotland to Newfoundland but was rapidly exterminated by man.

The main threat to many sea-birds now is from the increasing frequency of large-scale spillages of oil at sea. Few sea-birds that come into contact with the oil survive, diving birds such as guillemots and razorbills being the worst affected. Oiled birds collected from the coast and cleaned by well-wishers are often liberated in good health, but only a fraction of the birds reach any shore, and only a fraction of those that do are alive when they get there. Hence the praiseworthy efforts of those who clean oiled seabirds do little to reduce the threat to bird populations and neither the oil companies nor governments should be allowed to pretend that this is any remedy for the real problem. If present rates of oil spillage around southern Britain continue unchecked, there can be little doubt that our southern breeding populations of razorbill and guillemot will be lost.

Past increases in sea-bird numbers, especially fulmars, can be attributed to the development of the fishing industry, which provides them with extra food from whole fish or fish entrails discarded at sea. More recently, however, fishermen have found that declining fish stocks are affecting their livelihood and some sea-birds are also suffering from the overfishing. The clearest evidence of this is from sea-birds that depend on sand-eels off the Scottish coasts, such as arctic terns, but the effects may be much more widespread.